I0817423

THE THREE Rs

REDUCE, REUSE, AND RECYCLE

GLASS

Ruth Daly

Lightbox is an all-inclusive digital solution for the teaching and learning of curriculum topics in an original, groundbreaking way. Lightbox is based on National Curriculum Standards.

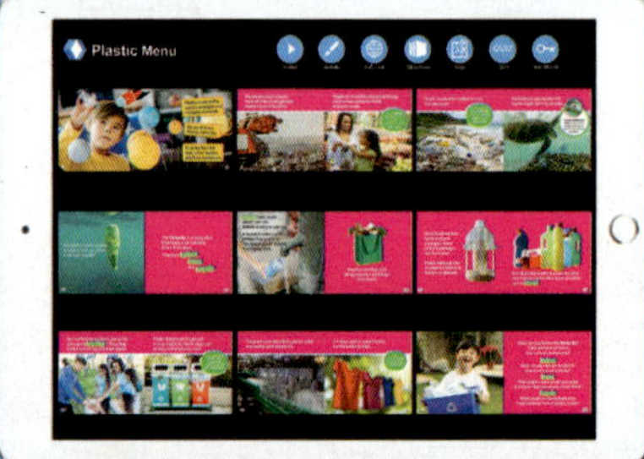

OPTIMIZED FOR

- ✓ **TABLETS**
- ✓ **WHITEBOARDS**
- ✓ **COMPUTERS**
- ✓ **AND MUCH MORE!**

STANDARD FEATURES OF LIGHTBOX

 **AUDIO** High-quality narration using text-to-speech system

 **VIDEOS** Embedded high-definition video clips

 **ACTIVITIES** Printable PDFs that can be emailed and graded

 **WEBLINKS** Curated links to external, child-safe resources

 **SLIDESHOWS** Pictorial overviews of key concepts

 **INTERACTIVE MAPS** Interactive maps and aerial satellite imagery

QUIZZES Ten multiple choice questions that are automatically graded and emailed for teacher assessment

 **KEY WORDS** Matching key concepts to their definitions

VIDEOS

WEBLINKS

SLIDESHOWS

QUIZZES

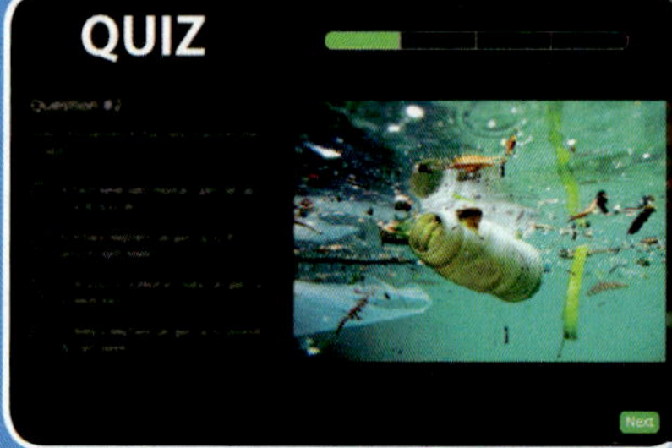

In this book, you will learn

what glass is,

how it affects Earth,

how it is wasted,

how you can help,

and much more!

Glass is a strong material that you can see through. Windows, cups, and mirrors are made of glass.

More than 40 billion glass containers are made in the United States each year.

These are mostly used for food and drinks.

We use more glass than we should. Bottles for drinks and jars for food are the kinds of glass we use most.

Much of the glass people use gets thrown away. This glass ends up broken in landfills.

The weight of all the glass bottles and jars we **throw out every year** is **heavier** than the **Great Pyramid of Giza.**

Glass waste often makes its way to rivers, lakes, and oceans. These bottles could still be there in a million years.

Some beaches have been used as garbage dumps in the past.

Glass Beach in California was once **a dump**. It is made up of **many pieces of colored glass**.

We can help keep glass out of landfills and water.

Everyone can help.

The **Three Rs** is an easy plan that helps us do just that. It has three steps.

These are reduce, reuse, and recycle.

We can **reduce** how much glass we use. Reduce means to use less.

We can use less glass if we buy bigger jars of food. The food can be put into small reusable containers at home.

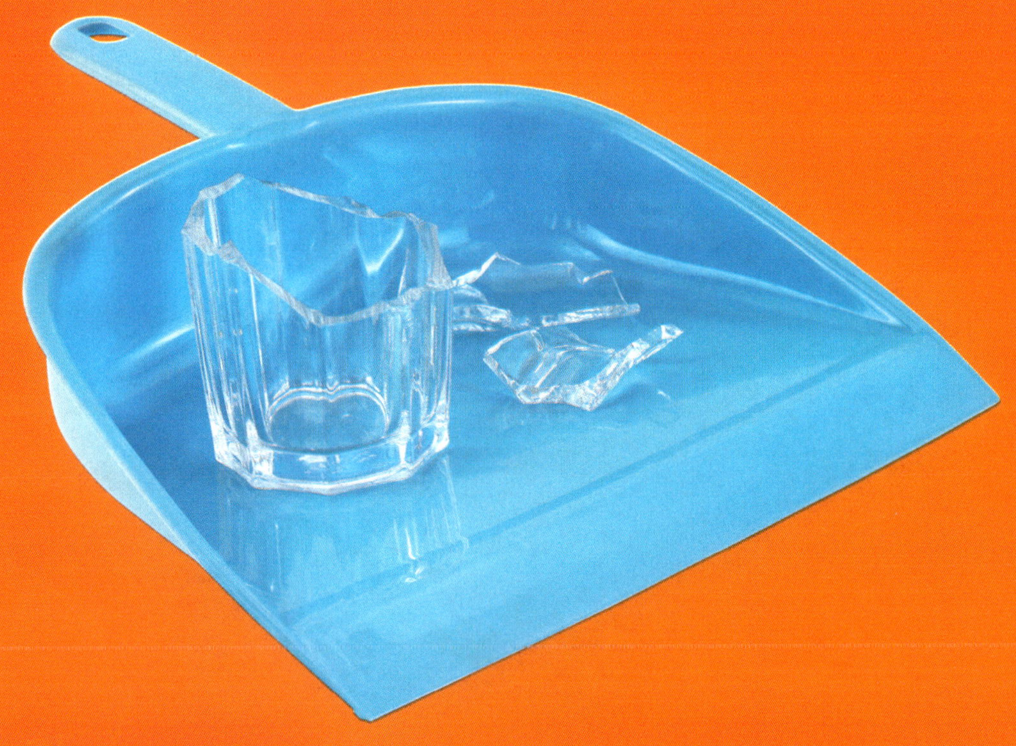

We can also take good care of the glass things we use at home. This means that we will not need to buy as many new glass things.

Glass jam jars can be **reused** in many ways.

They can be made into containers for plants. Some jars can be reused to store foods.

Broken glass is sharp. It can cut you. Always ask an adult to help you reuse glass in safe ways.

Recycling is the best way to keep glass out of the landfill. Recycling is when we make something new from used glass.

Bottles and jars can be put in recycling bins. Windows and light bulbs must be recycled in a different way.

We **save enough energy** to **power a TV** for **20 minutes** when we **recycle one glass jar**.

New glass bottles are made from the ones that we recycle.

It takes about **30 days** to **make a bottle** from **recycled glass.**

Recycled glass is also used to make fiberglass. Fiberglass fills the space inside walls to keep homes warm.

How can you follow the **Three Rs**? Think about your home, your school, and your neighborhood.

Reduce

How can you and your family use less glass?

Reuse

Can you think of different ways to reuse glass food containers at home?

Recycle

What steps could you take to keep glass out of the garbage at school?

GLASS FACTS

These pages provide detailed information that expands on the interesting facts found in the book. They are intended to be used by adults as a learning support to help young readers round out their knowledge of reducing, reusing, or recycling each kind of object or material featured in *The Three Rs* series.

Pages 4–5

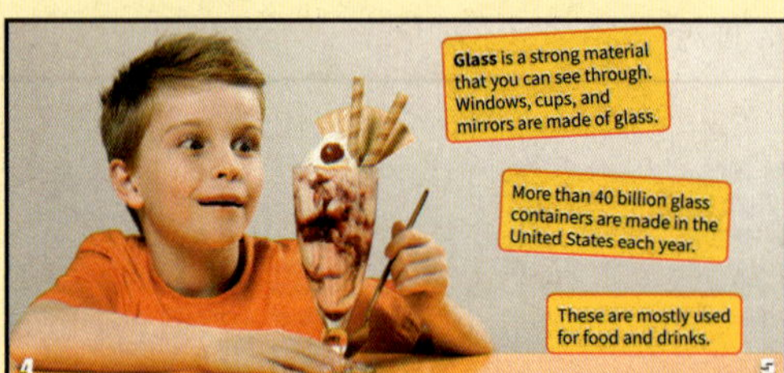

Glass has some useful properties. It is transparent, it does not conduct electricity, and it can be molded into shapes. Shaped glass containers are ideal for food and drinks. This is because glass keeps flavors in and bacteria out. Flat glass is used for windows because it lets the light in. It is also used to make walls and furniture. Glass can be used to make optical fibers that are used in medicine. It also used in reflective paint used on roads.

Pages 6–7

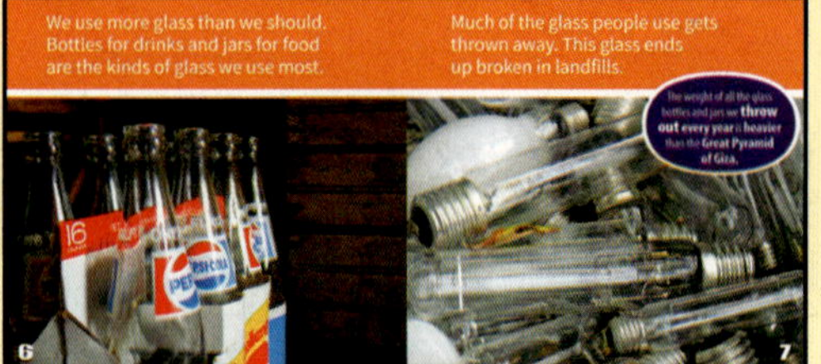

Glass takes up a large amount of space in landfills. People in the United States throw out about 10 million tons (9 million metric tons) of glass each year. Whether it is broken, crushed, or intact, glass can stay the same for thousands of years. Thankfully, glass does not contain harmful chemicals that could leach into the ground. However, it is still dangerous. Broken glass can cause injuries, and should always be cleaned up by an adult.

Pages 8–9

Some glass in the ocean is the result of shipwrecks. Other glass waste in the sea has made its way there by rivers. Glass like this may be hundreds of years old. When it washes up on the beach, it is called sea glass. Sea glass is partly see-through, and looks like glass pebbles. The pieces of glass have been eroded by the sea over many years, so the edges are not sharp. There are many glass beaches around the world. One well known glass beach is located in Hawai'i.

Pages 10–11

Most glass that we use in our homes can be easily reused and recycled. There are many organizations to help communities dispose of glass waste appropriately. These organizations give people ideas about the best ways they can recycle glass products they no longer want. They also help people understand why the Three Rs are important.

Pages 12–13

Glass is made by mixing sand with other minerals. This mixture is heated in a furnace to a high temperature before being set into shapes. People need to take care of the environment by using fewer natural resources. One way we can do this is to take better care of glass items we already have. This will reduce the amount of glass products we need to buy. As a result, there will be less demand on the natural resources that are required to produce glass.

Pages 14–15

Glass jars can be reused to store homemade jam. At home, glass bottles can be washed and reused to store liquids such as bath oils, pasta sauce, salad dressing, or juices. Glass containers used for storing any kind of food must be cleaned and sealed properly to prevent bacteria from getting into the food. Glass jars can be decorated and used in offices, or used to store nails and screws in a workshop.

Pages 16–17

Glass can be recycled many times without losing its qualities. Glass placed in the recycling should always be clean and should not be broken. Clear and colored glass should be separated. Some types of glass should be recycled separately from jars and bottles because they contain different chemicals. These include glass from windows, mirrors, ovenware, and light bulbs.

Pages 18–19

Recycled jars and bottles are made into new ones. This is called closed-loop recycling. The quality of recycled glass is the same as new glass made from natural resources. Less energy is required to recycle glass than to make it from scratch, which is better for the environment and climate. Glass may not ever decompose, so we should never throw it out. In fact, some glass artifacts have been found in Egypt that date back thousands of years.

Pages 20–21

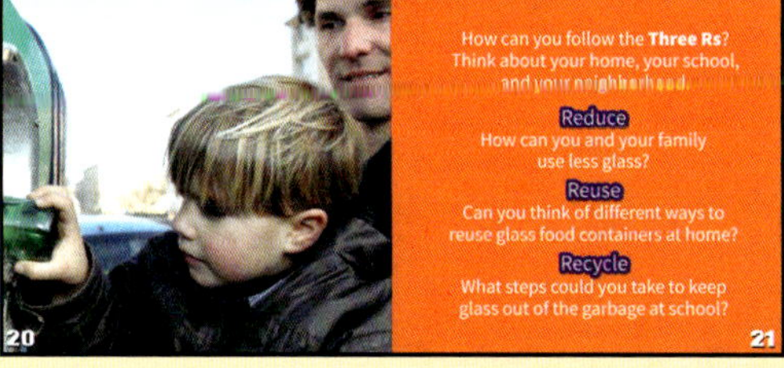

It might be difficult to reduce how much glass we use. However, we can look after the glass around us. By taking proper care of phones and tablets with glass screens, we will not need to replace them as often. Tell your family, friends, and classmates about the facts you have learned in this book. You could also start a craft club that reuses glass jars and bottles in your community. Why is it important to follow the Three Rs?

KEY WORDS

Research has shown that as much as 65 percent of all written material published in English is made up of 300 words. These 300 words cannot be taught using pictures or learned by sounding them out. They must be recognized by sight. This book contains 99 common sight words to help young readers improve their reading fluency and comprehension. This book also teaches young readers several important content words, such as proper nouns. These words are paired with pictures to aid in learning and improve understanding.

Page	Sight Words First Appearance
5	a, and, are, can, each, food, for, in, is, made, more, of, see, states, than, that, the, these, through, year, you
6	kinds, most, should, use, we
7	all, away, ends, every, gets, much, out, people, this, up
8	be, could, its, makes, often, rivers, still, there, to, way
9	as, been, have, it, many, once, some, was
10	help, keep, water
11	an, do, has, just, means, three, us
12	at, home, how, if, into, put, small
13	good, need, new, not, take, things, will
14	plants, they
15	always, ask, cut
16	from, something, when
17	different, enough, light, must, one
18	about, days,
19	also,
21	family, school, think, what, your

Page	Content Words First Appearance
5	containers, cups, drinks, glass, material, mirrors, United States, windows
6	bottles, jars
7	Giza, Great Pyramid, landfills
8	lakes, oceans, waste
9	beaches, California, dumps, Glass Beach, past
11	plan, recycle, reduce, reuse, steps, Three Rs
12	reusable containers
15	adult, sharp
17	energy, light bulbs, recycling bins, TV
19	fiberglass, space, walls
21	neighborhood

Published by Smartbook Media Inc.
350 5th Avenue, 59th Floor New York, NY 10118
Website: www.openlightbox.com

Library of Congress Control Number: 2018941513

ISBN 978-1-5105-3807-8 (hardcover)
ISBN 978-1-5105-3808-5 (multi-user eBook)

062018
120117

Printed in Brainerd, Minnesota, United States
1 2 3 4 5 6 7 8 9 0 22 21 20 19 18

Project Coordinator: Jared Siemens
Designer: Terry Paulhus

The publisher acknowledges Alamy, Getty Images, iStock, and Shutterstock as its primary image suppliers for this title.